Grades 9–12

Grammar Notebook
for
Punctuation, Capitalization, & Spelling

Understanding the Why's and How's of American English Grammar

Janelle Diller

These popular teacher resources and activity books are available from
ECS Learning Systems, Inc., and Novel Units, Inc.

ECS9676	Destinations	Grades 5-9
NU783XRH	Graphic Organizer Collection	Grades 3-12
ECS9501	Hemingway for Teachers	Grades 9-12
ECS9609	Inkblots	Grades 6-12
ECS0484	Not More Writing?!	Grades 9-12
ECS9633	Odysseys	Grades 5-9
ECS948X	Quick Thinking	Grades 7-12
ECS9706	Springboards for Reading	Grades 7-12
ECS0549	Structures for Reading, Writing, Thinking Book 1	Grades 4-9
ECS0557	Structures for Reading, Writing, Thinking Book 2	Grades 4-9
ECS0565	Structures for Reading, Writing, Thinking Book 3	Grades 4-9
ECS0573	Structures for Reading, Writing, Thinking Book 4	Grades 4-9
NU5958RH	Tackling Literary Terms	Grades 9-12
ECS9439	Tactics to Tackle Thinking	Grades 7-12
ECS9668	Voyages	Grades 5-9
ECS9080	Writing Warm-Ups	Grades 7-12
ECS9463	Writing Warm-Ups Two	Grades 7-12

To order, or for a complete catalog, write:

ECS Learning Systems, Inc.
P.O. Box 791439
San Antonio, Texas 78279-1439

Web site: www.educyberstor.com
or contact your local school supply store.

Editor: Shirley J. Durst
Cover Design and Page Layout: Anh N. Le

ISBN 1-57022-239-8

Printed in the United States of America.

Author's Note

I have a confession to make: I love grammar. Consequently, in most people's eyes, this makes me a little peculiar (I prefer the term "slightly eccentric," but I usually don't get to choose). If I have to name any single reason for why grammar fascinates me, it's because long ago I learned to enjoy the quirkiness of language. And English abounds in quirkiness. For instance, it's perfectly acceptable to ask: "I'm going with you, aren't I?" or "I'm going with you, am I not?" On the other hand, it's perfectly *unacceptable* to ask, "I'm going with you, are I not?" or "I'm going with you, amn't I?"

Infinitives present even more language quirkiness. In Latin (one of the root languages of English), infinitives literally cannot be "split" because in that language the infinitive form of a verb is a single word. As a result, some English language grammarians insist that infinitives should never be split. For example, using the infinitive *to double*, I would ordinarily say, "He plans *to more than double* his income by August." To keep from splitting the infinitive, I apparently *should* say, "He plans *more than to double* his income" or "He plans *to double more than* his income."

It is my belief that the joy felt in the exploration of a language is proportionate to how that language is eventually used. Consider the following analogy: Recently, I went to a Colorado Nuggets game with a young basketball fanatic friend of mine. Having a rudimentary understanding of how the game is played (ten people, one ball, big court, little basket), I enjoyed myself. My friend, however, was in ecstasy. He knew the statistics, strategies, potentials—every possible tidbit about each player and the overall game. I know that if I attended every game of the season with him, his knowledge would give me far greater enthusiasm for the sport.

The **Grammar Notebook** series is designed to give your students this kind of "courtside enthusiasm" for English grammar. The idea is for learners to start listening and observing, thinking and using the structure and rules of English in ways that they previously have not. Ultimately, as they begin to understand the "why's" of English grammar, they will be able to do the "how's." Whether they're trying to absorb a new grammar rule or change the way they speak and write, this is the best way to learn!

Janelle Diller

Janelle Diller

About the Author

Janelle Diller has taught high school, college, and workplace English, as well as directed the customized training division at Pikes Peak Community College (PPCC) in Colorado Springs, Colorado. Ms. Diller has developed curricula for workplace education which have been shared and adopted nationally. She has made presentations nationally and internationally on curriculum development and workplace education issues. Ms. Diller has also co-authored, with her husband, two books and a video for the construction industry. Her first novel, *For the Love of Gold* (Royal Fireworks Press) was selected as a Kansas State Reading Council choice in 1998-99.

Ms. Diller lives in Colorado Springs with her husband and two sons, who are all pleasantly tolerant of her love of grammar.

Table of Contents

The Grammar Notebook   ECS Learning Systems, Inc.

ECS Learning Systems, Inc.   The Grammar Notebook   **vii**

ECS Learning Systems, Inc.

Introduction

Beyond Drills and Prewritten Exercises

Famed Russian writer Isaac Babel once said, "No iron can pierce the heart with such force as a period put at just the right place." An exaggeration? Consider the stories told in the following identically-worded letters:

Dear John,

   I want a man who knows what love is all about. You are generous, kind, thoughtful. People who are not like you admit to being useless and inferior. You have ruined me for other men. I yearn for you. I have no feelings whatsoever when we're apart. I can be forever happy. Will you let me be yours?

Marsha

OR

Dear John,

   I want a man who knows what love is. All about you are generous, kind, thoughtful people who are not like you. Admit to being useless and inferior. You have ruined me. For other men, I yearn. For you, I have no feelings whatsoever. When we're apart, I can be forever happy. Will you let me be?

Yours,

Marsha

While you may not always produce as much drama with punctuation, it is important to understand that punctuation creates meaning and can change it as well. An equally important purpose of punctuation is to give direction to the reader. Noted writer Pico Iyer describes punctuation marks as "the road signs placed along the highway of our communication—to control speeds, provide directions, and prevent head-on collisions." Without punctuation or with incorrect punctuation, readers have to work much harder to understand the writer's meaning, and even then they may misinterpret it. The following pages will help you figure out which road signs you need and how to use them to write what you mean. No doubt, Marsha could learn a thing or two from these pages as well.

Although standard rules and explanations for punctuation, capitalization, and spelling are included, the focus of the **Grammar Notebook** series is shifted away from customary drills and toward helping learners develop a better understanding of the "why's" and "how's" of language conventions. The intent is to build thinking skills around why we follow certain conventions and to make the rules easier to learn and use.

Learning from Student Writing

As much as possible, punctuation, capitalization, and spelling should be taught and practiced within the context of students' own writing. This presents a challenge for the instructor. When grammar is taught with textbook or prewritten exercises, students may learn to recognize the concepts and still not be able to transfer what they've learned to their own writing. On the other hand, when teachers use only student work, instruction can seem disorganized and fragmented, with every aspect of grammar touched on but none explained completely.

The best approach is a combination of the two. In addition to prewritten exercises, students should always practice writing their own examples. They should also look for correct or incorrect examples in their everyday writing. To encourage this process, I've designed each book in the **Grammar Notebook** series to follow a simple teaching progression:

1. Explain each new concept to students, answering questions and giving lots of examples. (Use the chalkboard or transparencies to make points and to show example sentences.)

2. Work through the sample sentences in each section with students. This step gives you a window to what they understand and what they do not, as well as an opportunity to explain a concept from a new angle, if necessary.

3. Guide students in practicing the concepts by themselves, in pairs, or in groups. As an optional activity, have them examine their own work in other subject areas for examples of how they've correctly or incorrectly used a new concept. (To avoid hours of tedious grading, students can review each other's work in small groups, using the teacher for reference only.)

4. Encourage students to become aware of interesting uses of language. Have them learn and identify a minimum of three new words a week, describing how they learned each new word and how and when they used it (see page 77).

5. Encourage students to listen and read for usage errors on TV, radio, or in print. Have them identify what the correct usage should have been and whether the usage error was intentional. Follow up by having them describe the impact an intentional usage error may have had on the reader or listener (see page 78).

ECS Learning Systems, Inc.

What's Inside

To support the learning process described above, **Grammar Notebook** features the following:

- explanations of terms and/or rules

- examples that illustrate the terms and/or rules

- tips for remembering correct usage

- points for class or group discussion

- practice sentences for identifying correct usage

- exercises for practicing correct usage with students' own sentences

- a structure for student-led teaching of concepts

- a review of how students are applying what they've learned

- an opportunity for students to document what they have learned so far and to think about what they still want to learn

Finally, scattered throughout the text are sections entitled "Language Play." These sections make excellent discussion or essay starters. Each Language Play describes the lively and ever-changing nature of English and features opportunities for greater exploration of how our language is changing. The intent here is to awaken learners to the realization that not only does English continuously change, but that each of us is an active contributor to the ongoing metamorphosis.

Breaking the Traditional Teaching Mold

Education and sports—analogies abound.

Think for a few minutes of teachers and students in a traditional classroom situation as the pitcher and catcher on a baseball team. They're both on the same team and have common goals. The pitcher's purpose is to throw the ball; the catcher's is to catch it. As the ball flies through the air, somewhere between the pitcher and the catcher the responsibility shifts. The catcher is not responsible for the ball while it's still in the pitcher's hands. By the same token, the pitcher—even when the ball is poorly thrown—is not responsible for the ball once it is in the catcher's territory.

So it is in the traditional classroom. The teacher delivers information and students receive it. Once the teacher has "pitched" the information, it's up to the student to "catch" it. Somewhere in this process the responsibility shifts from teacher to student. Even if the information is poorly taught, the student is still responsible for knowing it.

ECS Learning Systems, Inc.   The Grammar Notebook

A better way to learn is for both teacher and student to take responsibility during the entire process. The earlier learners actively participate in the learning process, the more likely it is that they will truly understand the information and be able to apply it to something similar but not necessarily directly related. Likewise, the teacher's responsibility should not end as soon as the information has been delivered. If teachers go beyond traditional lines and expectations, students will be far more likely to understand, and, in the process, become better learners in general.

Teaching What You Know

Clearly, one of the most effective ways to learn something is to teach it. Schedule times for students to teach each other or reinforce concepts they're learning. Try a mix of the following teaching methods:

- Planned, but informal, lessons where students work in groups of two or three and take turns reinforcing or teaching concepts from the week to each other

- Spontaneous, five-minute lessons during class where students pair up and improve their understanding about something you've covered that day

To reduce student anxiety, students should begin with informal teaching sessions (see page 75). At least initially, don't grade on the quality of the lesson. As students' ability to explain concepts increases, offer them opportunities to share their spontaneous or informal lessons with the rest of the class.

Learning Styles

The **Grammar Notebook** series makes an effort to combine all three learning styles (auditory, visual, and kinesthetic) in both structured and nonstructured ways. As a teacher, you'll address both auditory and visual learning needs. The many practice and writing exercises included in **Grammar Notebook** are excellent for kinesthetic learning. These three learning styles are again reinforced as students are encouraged to listen to how others are using punctuation and spelling, watch for usages as they read, and teach others what they are learning (see page 76).

Conclusion

Most of all, remember to have fun with the subject. The rich history of English has created a language resonating with variety, texture, and color. If you, the teacher, can inspire students to grasp this, the rest will easily follow.

Before You Begin (For Students)...

Why Study Punctuation, Capitalization, and Spelling?

Without even being aware of it, people make subtle—and sometimes not so subtle—value judgments about others based on their language skills. If a person has a large vocabulary and follows standard rules, he or she is treated differently than someone whose vocabulary is limited or who ignores even basic grammar rules. As a result, people whose language skills aren't as polished or sophisticated as they should be are often passed over for job promotions—even when they have all the other necessary qualifications. This happens whether or not writing or oral skills are required to do the job well.

1. Think of a time when someone judged you either positively or negatively because of your grammar. Or think of a time when you judged someone favorably or unfavorably because of his or her grammar. Describe what happened and what you learned from the experience. Did the experience change you in any way?

2. What changes would you like to make in your writing?

3. On a separate sheet of paper, brainstorm every form of punctuation you can think of. Use more pages if necessary. Go back and put a check mark in front of the ones you understand how to use already.

4. List the questions you have about punctuation and spelling. What punctuation and spelling skills would you like to learn? As you learn more about punctuation and spelling, return to these pages to add new terms and skills and to check off the ones you have mastered.

Grammar Resources

List the resources you have for learning about grammar (books, people, places). Return to this list and add other helpful resources as you find them.

BOOKS

_____   _____
_____   _____
_____   _____
_____   _____
_____   _____

PEOPLE

_____   _____
_____   _____
_____   _____
_____   _____
_____   _____

PLACES

_____   _____
_____   _____
_____   _____
_____   _____

Punctuation

　　　　ECS Learning Systems, Inc.

 # Commas ,

Commas group words that belong together and separate words that do not belong together.

Place Markers in Numbers

Commas are used to distinguish number places (hundreds, thousands, millions, etc.).

> The lottery is up to $11,000,000.

Cities, States, and Countries

When the state or country is listed after the city, it is separated by a pair of commas. The state or country is treated like nonrestrictive material.

> Denver, Colorado, is the capital of Colorado.

Month, Day, and Year

When the month, day, and year are written out within a sentence, the year is separated by a pair of commas. When only the month and date or the month and year are given, do not use a comma.

> We'll meet March 6 to interview the last candidates.

> We'll meet in March 2005 to celebrate.

> We'll meet March 6, 2005, to celebrate.

Letter Greetings and Closings

Commas are used after the greeting and closing in a letter.

Dear Jane,

How are you? I am fine.

Sincerely,
Bob

Items in a Series

Items in a series can be nouns, verbs, phrases, and clauses. The comma before the *and* is optional. However, most writers continue to use a comma before the *and* to help keep the meaning clear.

My nieces, nephews, and cousins are a noisy bunch.

They laugh, chase, and swing from the chandelier at family gatherings.

Every time we get together, my mother threatens to hang them by their toes, feed them to the chickens, or stop feeding them so many cookies.

Extra Information

Commas group extra information.

Introductory information: *By the way*, Charles said he would be late.

Appositives: Aaron, *the neighbor's son*, is already driving.

Nonrestrictive information: Charles, *by the way*, said he would be late.

"Tagged-on" words: You're coming along, *aren't you*?

Commas with Quotations

After Quotation: "Books are good enough in their way, but they are a mighty bloodless substitute for life⊙" Robert Louis Stevenson once said.

Before Quotation: Robert Louis Stevenson once said⊙"Books are good enough in their way, but they are a mighty bloodless substitute for life."

Split Quotation: "Books are good enough in their way⊙" Robert Louis Stevenson once said⊙"but they are a mighty bloodless substitute for life."

ECS Learning Systems, Inc. The Grammar Notebook

No Commas

DO NOT separate the subject from the verb with a single comma.

No: How the Broncos blew it in the playoffs and missed their chance at the Superbowl⊙ is a mystery to their fans.

Yes: *How the Broncos blew it in the playoffs and missed their chance at the Superbowl* is a mystery to their fans. (The noun clause, which is bolded and italicized, functions as the subject.)

No: Kwanzaa which was created in 1966 in the wake of the Watts riots⊙ is an annual celebration of African-American heritage.

Yes: Kwanzaa⊙ *which was created in 1966 in the wake of the Watts riots*⊙ is an annual celebration of African-American heritage. (*Kwanzaa* is the subject. The relative clause, which is bolded and italicized, is nonrestrictive or extra material, which can be separated from the verb.)

DO NOT separate the verb from its object or subject complement with a single comma (except in the case of split direct quotations).

No: The seven principles of Kwanzaa are⊙ unity, self-determination, collective work and responsibility, cooperative economics, purpose, creativity, and faith.

Yes: The seven principles of Kwanzaa are unity, self-determination, collective work and responsibility, cooperative economics, purpose, creativity, and faith.

No: Over 13 million Americans celebrate at least in some way⊙ the seven-day celebration.

Yes: Over 13 million Americans celebrate⊙ *at least in some way*⊙ the seven-day celebration.

DO NOT separate the final adjective from the word it modifies.

No: She put on her cheeriest, most familiar⊙ hat to go to the meeting.

Yes: She put on her cheeriest⊙ most familiar hat to go to the meeting.

ECS Learning Systems, Inc.

It's Your Turn
Commas

■ Practice

Directions: On a separate sheet of paper, rewrite the following sentences, adding commas or deleting them where necessary.

1. Lisa's husband Brent is a good attorney isn't he?

2. "No one" Eleanor Roosevelt once said "can make you feel inferior without your consent."

3. On the other hand Mary would like to get the family together on July 3 instead of July 4.

4. The scientists known for studying insects were able to watch their behavior in close detail.

5. Sam left for London England with his best friend Ellen.

6. The kids built a really elaborate treehouse in the back yard and decorated it, with colored lights for Christmas.

7. March 15, 1994 was the last time we had more than two feet of snow from one storm.

8. In June 1996 the Bartels vacationed at the Grand Canyon hiked two mountains and had a family reunion.

9. Of all the books I read this summer I enjoyed *Stormy Weather* a black comedy the most.

10. Erin was born in Kelowna British Columbia wasn't she?

■ Write Your Own

Directions: On a separate sheet of paper, write sentences for the following prompts. Punctuate properly.

1. A city and state

2. A month, day, and year named together

3. Only two of the following three: month, day, or year

4. A series of phrases

5. Introductory information

6. An appositive

7. Nonrestrictive information

8. "Tagged-on" words

9. "Tagged-on" words

10. A quote

ECS Learning Systems, Inc.

Quotation Marks " "

Quotation marks mark the beginning and end of directly quoted words.

Direct Quotations

A **quotation** is the writer's or speaker's exact words. In a **direct quotation**, the speaker's words are reported exactly as they were originally written or spoken and are enclosed with quotation marks. When writing direct quotations, pay special attention to where the commas and periods go. In the first two sentences below, the verb *said* is separated from the quotation with a comma.

> Tallulah Bankhead said, "If I had my life to live again, I'd make the same mistakes, only sooner."

The first letter of the word after a **split quotation** is never capitalized unless it is ordinarily capitalized, as in the word *I'd* in the following sentence.

> "If I had my life to live again," Tallulah Bankhead said, "I'd make the same mistakes, only sooner."

Notice, too, that any end punctuation connected to the quote falls *inside* the quotation marks:

> "If I had my life to live again, I'd make the same mistakes, only sooner," Tallulah Bankhead said.

Quotations within a Sentence

To blend **direct quotations** into a sentence, put quotation marks around the direct quotations, only. Do not capitalize the first letter of the first word of the blended quotations unless it would ordinarily be capitalized.

> Rose Macaulay says you should believe everything in the newspapers, since "this makes them more interesting."

ECS Learning Systems, Inc. The Grammar Notebook

Indirect Quotations

An indirect quotation reports someone's ideas without using his or her exact words. Quotation marks are not used around indirect quotations, as in the sentences below.

> Tallulah Bankhead claims that if she could live her life again, she'd make the same mistakes. The difference is she'd make them sooner.

Quotations within Quotations

Single quotation marks enclose a quotation within a quotation:

> Somerset Maughm said, "It wasn't until quite late in life that I discovered how easy it is to say, 'I don't know.'"

Titles

Quotation marks are placed around the titles of short works: newspaper and magazine articles, poems, short stories, songs, episodes of television and radio programs, and chapters or subdivisions of books. Titles of books, plays, and films and the names of magazines and newspapers are italicized (or underlined, if the sentence title is handwritten).

> Did you read "A Challenge the Schools Didn't Take" in *US News*?

Quotation marks may be used to set off examples of particular words. In print, the words may be bolded or italicized, instead. (Whichever style you choose, be consistent.)

> Former Vice President Dan Quayle misspelled *potato* when he visited an elementary school.

Quotation Marks with Other Punctuation

Periods and commas always go *inside* the quotation marks, even if they don't seem to logically belong there.

> One of my favorite essays is James Thurber's "University Days."

Colons and semicolons go *outside* the quotation marks.

> The prize for the best paper went to "Drucker's Influence on Management"; it was the only paper submitted.

Question marks, exclamation points, and dashes go *inside* or *outside*, depending on whether they belong with the quoted material or with the sentence as a whole.

> Did you hear him read "The Road Not Taken"?

> Did you hear him ask, "Who is ready for lunch?"

It's Your Turn
Quotation Marks

■ Practice

Directions: On a separate sheet of paper, rewrite the sentences below, correcting capitalization errors and adding quotation marks and commas.

1. Kathy Norris claims in spite of the cost of living, it's still popular.

2. One time the police stopped me for speeding and they said don't you know the speed limit is 55 miles per hour? I said yeah, I know, but I wasn't gonna' be out that long. —*Steven Wright*

3. It is not the strongest of the species that survive, nor the most intelligent Charles Darwin said but the one most responsive to change.

4. Brian Kiley announced I went to a bookstore the other day. I asked the woman behind the counter where the self-help section was. She said if I told you that, it would defeat the whole purpose.

5. Last night Ron Fairly stated during on-air coverage of a San Francisco Giants game I neglected to mention something that bears repeating.

6. This taught me a lesson, but I'm not sure what it is John McEnroe once stated after losing a championship game.

7. Albert Szent-Gyorgyi points out that discovery is nothing more than *an accident meeting a prepared mind*. [quoted portion in italics]

8. I merely took the energy it takes to pout Duke Ellington said and wrote some blues.

9. Proofreading is like scrimshaw James J. Kilpatrick laments. It is getting to be a lost art.

10. Peter de Vries loves being a writer, even though he can't stand the paperwork.

■ Write Your Own

Directions: On a separate sheet of paper, write sentences for the following prompts.

1. Enclose a direct quotation in quotation marks.

2. Paraphrase a quote.

3. Enclose a quotation within a quotation.

4. Include the title of a song at the end of the sentence.

5. Use a semicolon immediately after the title of a poem.

6. Use quotation marks to set off examples of particular words.

7. Blend a quote into a sentence.

8. Include the title of a newspaper article.

9. End a question with the title of a song you like.

10. Enclose a direct quotation. Separate the quote into two parts and identify the speaker in between the two parts.

ECS Learning Systems, Inc.

Language Play:
The Most Commonly Used Words

How many words are there in the English language? It's impossible to get an exact count, for many reasons. But a logical place to start, at least, is with dictionaries. The 1989 *Revised Oxford English Dictionary* includes 615,000 entries, but this barely touches the potential real number. One reason it's so hard to determine the actual number is because words have so many different meanings. Take, for instance, the word *cool*, which can be an adjective or a verb. Consider the following usages given by the *1991 American Heritage Dictionary*:

cool weather
a *cool* breeze
a *cool* head in a crisis
a *cool* greeting
a *cool* look
a *cool* color
a *cool* kid
a *cool* million
cooled his passion
cool off
cool as a cucumber
the *cool* of the morning
recovered her *cool*
cool your heels
cool it

Is *cool* a single word or 15 words? Even with all these definitions, what definitions are missing?

To further complicate getting an accurate word count, how do we treat words like *surprise* and *surprize*? Both mean the same thing but are simply spelled differently. Do they count as one word or two? And what about all the scientific and technical terms not found in the traditional dictionary? Think of all the medical terms, the various names of flora and fauna—there are 1.4 million named insect species alone (at least 0.4 million of which tend to show up on the average camping weekend). Considering this, the best estimates for the number of words in the English language start at several million and move up from there.

ECS Learning Systems, Inc.

Perhaps a more important question is how many words does the average person know and use? This, too, is difficult to answer. Different scholars have counted the number of words in the King James version of the Bible and estimate the number to be between 7,000 and 10,442. Other scholars estimate Shakespeare used between 16,000 and 30,000 words. Even these numbers don't tell us a lot because we all know far more words than we ever might put into writing. (For instance, we all know what *cowabunga* means, but most of us have never had the opportunity or courage to put it in one of our essays.)

Various linguists estimate an average vocabulary to be somewhere between 15,000 words and 250,000. With this range of guesses, we can safely assume no one really knows. It is, however, somewhat easier to determine the number of words commonly used in print by examining books, newspapers, and so on. In 1923, just such an extensive study was done by G. H. McKnight, a lexicographer. He determined that 43 words account for half of all the frequently used words. And just nine words comprise a full quarter of the words used most in writing.

Explore

A. What do you think were the nine most commonly written words in English in 1923? Keep in mind that this list reflects written language rather than spoken language. Will the list, therefore, be comprised of common words in formal or informal language usage? Will this make a difference in which words are most commonly used? How might the list be different if McKnight had only recorded and tabulated conversational words? Formal speeches? Radio announcers?

   1. What part of speech will the words most likely be? Nouns, pronouns, verbs, adjectives, adverbs, prepositions, conjunctions, or interjections? Why?

   2. Think about your own writing (or pull out an example and do a quick word count). What are the most common words used? Do you think this is typical?

   3. McKnight's study was done in 1923. Do you think the words on the list would have changed in the last 70 years? Why or why not? If they might have changed, what kinds of words would move out of and into common usage?

ECS Learning Systems, Inc.

B. These are the nine words McKnight determined were the most written in 1923:

and, be, have, it, of, the, to, will, you

With the advent of computers, McKnight's efforts are easily duplicated. Collins Birmingham University International Language Database (COBUILD), which is owned by HarperCollins, has created a computer-concordanced dictionary of English. Using a corpus of 200 million words of running text, COBUILD is able to document subtle shifts in language usage with a few quick keystrokes. In 1996, COBUILD produced this list of the nine words most frequently used in writing in order of usage: *the, of, and, to, a, in, that, I, it.*

1. Compare the two lists. List the words both have in common.

2. The first list has three verbs (*be, have, will*). The second list doesn't have any. Why do you think this is true?

3. The 1923 list includes *you*; the 1996 list has *I.* Is there any significance in this?

4. How did your list vary from this? Are your choices more logical? Why or why not? Do some of these words surprise (or surprize) you?

5. Since COBUILD's work is descriptive rather than prescriptive, how might this impact acceptable usage?

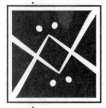

Colons :

Colons are used after independent clauses to direct attention to a list, an **appositive** (a word or phrase that renames or describes a noun or pronoun), or a quotation. *Don't* capitalize the first word of the list or the appositive. *Do* capitalize the first word of the quotation.

> **List:** We plan to visit all the great tourist spots: the Garden of the Gods, Pikes Peak, and Barney's Diner.

> **Appositive:** His laundry pile could be described in two words: *big* and *smelly*.

> **Direct Quotation:** Consider the advice Clark Kehrwald Cook gives to writers: "An Eskimo carver selects a promising stone, studies it to see what figure it suggests, then chips away at it to free the desired form; you can approach your draft in much the same way."

Colons are also used between independent clauses if the second clause summarizes or explains the first. The first word in the second independent clause may be capitalized or may be left in lower case. Just be consistent throughout your material.

> Faith is like love: It cannot be forced.

■ Tip

An independent clause *always* comes before a colon. What comes after the colon may be, but doesn't have to be, an independent clause. The most common error with colons is using one after the verb as in the following:

> **Incorrect:** Please bring: a sleeping bag, sturdy hiking shoes, and a flashlight.

> **Correct:** Please bring a sleeping bag, sturdy hiking shoes, and a flashlight.

To test, cover up whatever follows the colon. If whatever comes *before* the colon is a sentence, the colon is correctly placed. If what remains isn't a complete idea, the colon is not correctly used.

ECS Learning Systems, Inc.

■ Discuss

The use of colons is changing. As you read, write examples of how colons are used incorrectly. Identify the publications where you've found mistakes. What are common misuses? What kinds of publications misuse colons?

How do you think this usage will impact rules about colons? (For instance, if a small-town newspaper consistently uses a colon after verbs, would this have the same impact as in a national magazine?)

What other punctuation errors do you see in print? Do you see any pattern? Do you think any of these will eventually impact usage rules?

What errors do you have the most trouble with?

Semicolons ;

Semicolons are used in place of a period to indicate a close relationship between independent clauses. They are also used as a substitute for commas to improve clarity.

Independent Clauses

Semicolons are used when independent clauses closely related in meaning are not joined by a coordinating conjunction.

> I don't know who my grandfather was; I am much more concerned to know what his grandson will be. —*Abraham Lincoln*

Semicolons are used between independent clauses linked with a conjunctive adverb or transitional phrase.

> Sandy plans to travel to Jamaica over spring break; however, she still hasn't bought an airline ticket.

Items in a Series

Semicolons are used between items in a series containing internal punctuation. They are also used to separate phrases in a series or to separate items that already contain commas.

> I have lived in Hesston, Kansas; Goshen, Indiana; and Colorado Springs, Colorado.

■ Tip

Except for using a semicolon between items in a series, there should always be an independent clause *before* and *after* the semicolon. To test, cover up everything that comes *after* the semicolon. Is it a complete sentence? Now cover up everything that comes *before* the semicolon. Is it a complete sentence? If the answer is *yes* to both questions, the semicolon is correct. If the answer is *no* to either question, do not use a semicolon. A colon or a comma would work instead.

> **No:** I can't even clear my throat in five minutes; much less introduce the next president.

> **Yes:** I can't even clear my throat in five minutes, much less introduce the next president. —*Jack Kemp*

> **Yes:** I can't even clear my throat in five minutes, much less introduce the next president; I won't even try.

ECS Learning Systems, Inc.   The Grammar Notebook

It's Your Turn
Commas, Colons, and Semicolons

Directions: On a separate sheet of paper, rewrite the following sentences to correct comma, colon, and semicolon errors.

Everyone is brilliant some of the time: and no one is that way all the time.
—*Kathleen Cashes*

Everyone is brilliant some of the time, and no one is that way all the time.
—or—
Everyone is brilliant some of the time; no one is that way all the time.

1. Great assets are: talent, intelligence, facility, and opportunity.

2. When your habits reflect your intentions; the world will see you as yourself.
—*Greg Henry Quinn*

3. Failure like success is the result of an attempt.

4. Don't regret your mistakes, instead, regret your missed opportunities to correct them.

5. Carl Jung said: "The meeting of two personalities is like the contact of two chemical substances, if there is any reaction, both are transformed."

6. Govern a family as you would fry small fish; gently. —*Chinese Proverb*

7. A divorce is like an amputation, you survive, but there's less of you. —*Margaret Atwood*

8. Writing is the only thing that when I do it; I don't feel I should be doing something else.
—*Gloria Steinem*

9. To be loved: be lovable. —*Ovid*

10. I see but one rule, to be clear. If I am not clear: all my world crumbles to nothing.
—*Marie Henri Beyle Stendhal*

ECS Learning Systems, Inc.

■ Write Your Own

Directions: On a separate sheet of paper, write sentences for the following prompts.

1. A colon beginning a list

2. A colon directing attention to an appositive

3. A colon beginning a quote

4. A colon separating two independent clauses

5. A semicolon separating two independent clauses

6. A semicolon and transition word or phrase separating two independent clauses

7. Semicolons separating items in a series containing internal punctuation

8. Semicolons between long and involved items in a series

9. Semicolons separating three independent clauses

10. A transition word or phrase separating two independent clauses

ECS Learning Systems, Inc.   The Grammar Notebook

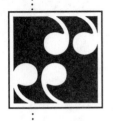

Apostrophes '

Apostrophes confuse writers because they have two important—but very different—functions. They are used in contractions to replace missing letters or numbers. They are also used to show possession.

Missing Letters and Numbers

Apostrophes show the omission of numerals and letters.

they are	you are	it is	going	1990
they're	you're	it's	goin'	'90

Clinton was elected in **'92**.

The little train went **chuggin'** up the hill.

Apostrophes are *no longer* necessary to make numerals and single letters plural. However, an apostrophe may be added to avoid confusion. Whichever you choose, remember to be consistent.

My son made all **A's** this last semester.

I have four **ds** in my name.

The **'60s** were turbulent times.

Possession

Apostrophes are also used to show possession. To test whether you have added the apostrophe correctly, cover up the **'** or **'s** with your finger. The word that is left should be the nonpossessive form of the word you want. For instance, where does the apostrophe go in the following sentence?

My cousins car is in the drive.
(Do you mean the car of one cousin or the car of two or more cousins?)

My *cousin's* car is in the drive.

cousin's = the car of one cousin
cousins' = the car of two (or more) cousins

ECS Learning Systems, Inc.

An additional way to test for correct punctuation is to rewrite the sentence with the possessive word in a prepositional phrase that shows ownership. This reveals whether the singular form of the word ends in **s**.

Put the ***childrens*** toys away.

No: Put the toys of the ***childrens*** away.

Yes: Put the toys of the ***children*** away.

Childrens is not a word, so the apostrophe must be placed between the **n** and the **s**.

Put the ***children's*** toys away.

Singular Possessive

Use an apostrophe plus **s** to form the singular possessive.

Jane's books were left at home. (the books belonging to Jane)

Today's world is dangerous. (the world of today)

It's all part of a ***day's*** work. (the work of a day)

The ***U.S.A.'s*** Olympic team won the diving competition. (the Olympic team of the U.S.A.)

■ Tip

When a singular noun ends in **s**, you may add an apostrophe only or add an apostrophe plus **s**. If by adding **'s** the word becomes difficult to pronounce or a new syllable is created, add only the apostrophe. With two-syllable words such as *Charles or Kansas*, it's common to add only the apostrophe. (Whatever you do, be consistent!)

Bob ***Jones's*** car is a 1976 Mustang. (the car belonging to Bob Jones)

Kansas' weather is volatile. (weather typical of Kansas)

Plural Possessive

Most plural nouns end in **s**. Just add an apostrophe for the possessive form.

> The *girls'* coats were warm. (the coats belonging to the girls.)

> Her *friends'* expressions of concern warmed her heart. (the expressions of her friends; notice that her friends have more than one expression.)

When a plural does not end in **s**, add **'s**.

> That store sells inexpensive *women's* hats. (the hats for women)

> The *chairmen's* notes were different from their committee members' notes. (the notes belonging to the chairmen)

> The *CPAs'* meeting was the longest. (the meeting the CPAs held)

Joint Possession

Add an apostrophe to only the last name when there is joint possession. Add an **'s** to both if there is separate possession.

> *Bob* and *Tom's* room is a mess. (the room that Bob and Tom share)

> *John's* and *Ted's* test scores were in the top 5%. (John's test is separate from Ted's test.)

Compound Nouns

If a noun is compound, use **'s** (or **s'**) with the last element in the compound.

> My *mother-in-law's* quilts are beautiful. (the quilts belong to my mother-in-law)

> My *sisters-in-law's* children are all smart. (the children belong to my two [or more] sisters-in-law)

■ Tip

> Even if you've used the correct form, it may sound awkward. If it sounds too strange, rewrite the sentence so it does not require a possessive and is still grammatically acceptable.
>
> The children of my *sisters-in-law* are all smart.

    ECS Learning Systems, Inc.

Indefinite Pronouns

Use **'s** to show that an indefinite pronoun is possessive.

> *Someone's* books are on the table. (the books belonging to someone)

■ Tip

> Avoid misuses of the apostrophe. Do *not* use apostrophes with nouns simply because they end in **s**. Do not use an apostrophe with possessive pronouns: *its, ours, yours, theirs, hers, his, and whose.*

Confusing Homonyms

It is common for writers to confuse the spelling and punctuation of certain homonyms (words that sound the same but have different spellings and meanings). The best way to remember which to use is to memorize each homonym and its usage.

Word	Usage	Example
it's	a contraction for *it is*	*It's* raining.
its	a possessive pronoun	The dog hurt *its* paw.
they're	a contraction for *they are*	*They're* happy to be home.
their	a possessive pronoun	This is *their* home.
there	an adverb that refers to a place or position.	The cookies are over *there*.
who's	a contraction for *who is*	*Who's* coming with us?
whose	a possessive pronoun	*Whose* book is this?
you're	a contraction for *you are*	*You're* first in line.
your	a possessive pronoun	*Your* books are on the table.

ECS Learning Systems, Inc.   The Grammar Notebook

It's Your Turn
Apostrophes

Directions: Circle the apostrophe errors in the following sentences. Write the correct form underneath the incorrect word form.

In the 60's, Colorado Springs city council decided to drop the apostrophe in Pike's Peak.
'60s   Springs'

1. Id like to know who's idea it was to change the rules, probably someones brother-in-laws.

2. Changing grammar rules sound's like something from the 1960's.

3. Im surprised they didnt decide to do away with quotation marks' while they were at it.

4. Its' a good thing they havent tried to legislate other grammar rules.

5. Apostrophes cause writers headaches! After a while, it looks like all the **s'** need one.

6. Jess and Tom's essays show the boys' trouble with apostrophes' may never end.

7. Its really not as difficult as it looks; with a few hours practice, most people can understand the rule's.

8. Just remember, look for missin letters and words that show possession.

9. Jess' and Tom's teacher has answered their' apostrophe questions.

10. It's hotter now than it was in the early '50's.

The Grammar Notebook   ECS Learning Systems, Inc.

■ Write Your Own

Directions: On a separate sheet of paper, follow the prompts and write sentences using apostrophes.

Write a sentence describing the dogs owned by Bess and Jess.

Jess's dog is bigger than *Bess's* dog. (Jess owns a dog, and Beth owns a dog.)
—**or**—
Jess and *Bess's* dogs sleep in the garage. (They *both* own the same dogs.)

1. Use an indefinite pronoun that shows ownership.

2. Show joint possession of a house.

3. Show that the Barnes and Bartel families each own a red car.

4. Use *its* and *it's*.

5. Describe the kitchens of your sisters-in-law.

6. Describe the clerks at the grocery store.

7. Use an apostrophe form you have trouble with.

8. Use *you're* and *your*.

9. Use *their* and *they're*.

10. Show that Ann and Bess share a bike.

ECS Learning Systems, Inc.   The Grammar Notebook

End Punctuation . ? !

Every sentence ends with punctuation: a period, an exclamation mark, or a question mark.

. = Declarative sentences (those that make a statement) and imperative commands end with a period.

? = Interrogative sentences (those that ask a question) end with a question mark.

! = Emphatic words, phrases, or statements end with an exclamation mark.

While this seems simple enough, not everyone uses end punctuation correctly. When in doubt, use the following as guidelines.

1. Use a **period** if the sentence reports a question rather than asks a question.

   Mom asked if I liked the creamed spinach ⊙

2. Use a **period** or **exclamation mark** after an **interrogative sentence** or **command**, depending on your meaning.

   Bring me the book ⊙

   Bring me the book ①

3. Use a **question mark** for **polite requests**.

   Could you bring dessert ⑦

ECS Learning Systems, Inc.

4. Use a **question mark** with a **confirmatory remark**.

    You're going with us, aren't you ⑦

5. Use a **question mark** after **questions in a series** even if the questions aren't complete sentences. Capitalize the first letter of each word grouping.

    What do you dream of becoming ⑦ A teacher ⑦ A dancer ⑦ The President ⑦

6. **Avoid overusing exclamation marks**. The more often you use an exclamation mark, the less impact it has. For instance, the following sentence is forceful enough without an exclamation mark.

    No matter how many times I replay the memory in my mind, I can't change the events ⊙

7. **Use only one end punctuation mark at a time**. Do not use multiple exclamation marks or an exclamation mark and question mark together. If you find you have to use multiple exclamation marks to convey the impact, rewrite the sentence itself so that it's clear and forceful enough with a single mark.

8. If a sentence ends with an abbreviation that uses periods, **do not add a second period**.

    We'll leave for the airport at 6:00 a.m ⊙ That should get us there in plenty of time.

Other Punctuation Marks

Dashes -- —

Dashes emphasize information in a dramatic way. In handwriting, two hyphens (--) are used to form a dash. Do not leave a space on either side of the dash. In computer word processing, the **em-dash** (—), a computer keyboard symbol the length of three hyphens, replaces the handwritten dash. There are no spaces on either side of the em-dash.

Nonrestrictive Information

Use dashes in a sentence to draw attention to nonrestrictive (unnecessary) information. Be careful not to overuse them, or they quickly lose their effectiveness.

> It is never too late—in spite of what others may tell you—to be what you might have been.

Appositives

Dashes set off appositives that contain commas:

> The Three Stooges—Larry, Curley, and Moe—continue to entertain children and irritate mothers.

Dramatic Shift

Dashes prepare the reader for a dramatic shift in tone or thought, significant list, or amplification. Again, avoid overuse, or the dash will lose its impact.

> Insanity is hereditary—you get it from your children. —*Sam Levenson*

Warning: Avoid using a dash just because you're unsure of what the correct punctuation is.

Parentheses ( )

Parentheses separate certain information from the rest of the sentence. Their function is similar, but slightly different, to that of commas, since they disrupt the flow of words for the reader more than commas do. Each time you use parentheses, consider whether the disruption will impede the readability and impact of what you've written. As with the dash, avoid overuse.

> Dusty prefers playing classical music (Bach, Chopin, Beethoven, among others) to jazz.

Numbers and Letters in a Series

Numbers or letters marking items in a series can be put in parentheses.

> The witnesses were asked to report three things: (1) what they saw, (2) who left the scene of the crime, and (3) which suspect had called the police.

Punctuation within Parentheses

Punctuation usually falls outside of the parentheses unless it is part of the material inside the parentheses.

> **Inside:** Every day the assignment includes (are you ready for this?) 30 math problems and 20 sentences to diagram.

> **Outside:** Whenever you get discouraged (as everyone does from time to time), remember that this, too, shall pass.

Brackets [ ]

Use **brackets** for letters or words you have changed or added to an otherwise word-for-word quotation. Use only for clarification. Never use brackets to change the author's meaning.

> *US News* reports, "[RU-486] is a legendary pill, miraculous to those who want it, murderous to those who hate it."

Use the Latin word *sic*, meaning "thus" or "so," in brackets to signify an error or change in the original source. Do not overuse, as in the sentence below. This can appear snobbish, particularly if attention to the error is small or could have been avoided by paraphrasing the original quotation.

> The spelling champion wrote to the editor complaining that the paper "does a terrible job of proofreading for mispelled **[sic]** words."

Ellipsis...

The **ellipsis mark** consists of three periods with spaces before the first period and after the last period. It is used to show that a full sentence or part of a sentence has been deleted from a quotation. It is also used to show an unfinished thought.

■ Tip

> In computerized word processing, a particular computer keystroke is used to produce the ellipsis. This symbol appears as a series of three periods with no spaces between (...).

Deleted Partial Sentence

The ellipsis mark is used to show that you have deleted a word or words from a quotation. As with brackets, *never* use the ellipsis mark to change the author's meaning.

> Prejudices...are most difficult to eradicate from the heart whose soil has never been loosened or fertilized by education. —*Charlotte Brontë*

Deleted Full Sentence

Use a period before the three periods when you've deleted a full sentence or more in the middle of the quotation. Notice there is no space before the first period.

> "The strategy is shrewd.⊙⊙ The company would like to be known as an information provider, as a bearer of medical alternatives, not as an entity with a profit margin."
>   —*US News & World Report*

Ellipsis Mark with Quotations

Do not use the ellipsis mark at the beginning of a quotation. The reader already assumes that something may have come before the quoted material. Likewise, do not use it at the end of a quotation unless you have deleted words from the final sentence.

Use the ellipsis mark to show a pause or unfinished thought. Again, do not overuse!

> As Maria lay dying, she whispered to Juan, "I've always loved you, but even more, I've loved ⊙⊙"

Hyphens -

Hyphens consist of a single dash. Do not leave space on either side of the hyphen.

Use a hyphen to connect two or more words acting together as an adjective *before* a noun. Do not use a hyphen if they come *after* a noun.

> **Before a noun:** Any mother could perform the jobs of several *air-traffic* controllers with ease. —*Lisa Alther*

> **After a noun:** The controllers handle *air traffic*.

■ Tip

> In a series of hyphenated words, "suspend" the hyphen.

> > The *first-, second-,* and *third-row* tickets are all sold out.

> Do not use hyphens to connect *-ly* adverbs to adjectives.

> > The *loudly barking* dog annoyed the neighbors.

Hyphenated Compound Words

Use a hyphen when writing numbers twenty-one through ninety-nine and for fractions.

> *Three-fourths* of my students are older than *twenty-five*.

Check a dictionary to determine if a compound word should be a hyphenated compound, unhyphenated compound, or two words.

Use a hyphen with the prefixes *self-*, *all-*, and *ex-* (when it means former), and with the suffix *-elect*.

> The Wizard Carnac is *all-knowing*, yet a model of *self-restraint*.

Use a hyphen between prefixes and base words that have duplicate letters or may have multiple meanings.

> The *anti-independence* movement is losing steam.

> A Passion Play is a *re-creation* of the last days of Christ.

> *Recreation* is as necessary as food for a healthy life.

Rules for Dividing Words

Use a hyphen to separate syllables of a word continued on another line.

— Divide words between syllables.

— Divide the word so that more than one letter is left at the end of a line and more than three letters begin the next line.

— Divide only words with two or more syllables.

— Divide compound words only between the words, not the syllables in the compound.

■ Discuss

As computer technology influences virtually every area of our lives, punctuation styles and rules in word processing are affected, as well. What changes in punctuation rules and styles have you noticed? When or where have you noticed these changes? Do you think these changes are beneficial? Why or why not?

The Grammar Notebook   ECS Learning Systems, Inc.

It's Your Turn
Punctuation

Directions: On a separate sheet of paper, rewrite the following sentences, correcting the punctuation.

1. Some of the smaller cities in Colorado, Colorado Springs, Pueblo, and Grand Junction, resent paying for roads in Denver—when improvements are also needed in these smaller cities.

2. Consequently rush hour traffic has grown into an unbearable snarl in Colorado Springs [according to regular commuters.]

3. But maybe it's a blessing (in disguise;) better roads bring more people—and the smaller cities are already growing fast enough.

4. Even if the state has no money to expand the highway system, the forty year old road system in Colorado still needs an over-haul.

5. Potholes, narrow bridges, and too few lanes all create hazards for even wary travelers.

6. If drivers are lucky enough to avoid accidents…they still risk blowing tires and wrecking alignments on the hazard packed highways.

7. The Colorado-highway department claims that they have a greater disadvantage over most states—they have to build mountains roads.

8. Mountain highways can cost twenty five-times as much as building highways on the plains, which puts pressure on the ever shrinking construction-dollar.

9. Add this to the state's much admired determination to restore the surrounding land back to its original state—and it's no wonder the rest of the state feels cheated.

10. One legislator—who is not known as a defender of the environment—complained that "…taking the land back to its original state is bad enough, but do we have to make it even better than it was? That's outrageously ex-pensive!…"

ECS Learning Systems, Inc.   The Grammar Notebook

■ Write Your Own

Directions: On a separate sheet of paper, write sentences for the following prompts.

1. Dashes drawing attention to nonrestrictive (unnecessary) material

2. Dashes setting off appositives that contain commas

3. Parentheses separating parenthetical explanations or supplemental material

4. Numbers or letters in a series

5. Brackets denoting letters or words that have been changed or added to a quote

6. The ellipsis mark denoting deletions from a quote

7. A hyphen connecting two or more words acting together as an adjective

8. A fraction written out in words

9. A number between 21 and 99 written out in words

10. Punctuation within parentheses

The Grammar Notebook   ECS Learning Systems, Inc.

Language Play: Adding New Words

As we've already discovered, it's impossible to pinpoint the number of words in the English language. Nor can we determine how large a person's vocabulary is, in part because we understand so many shades of meaning for most of the words we know, far more than any dictionary can ever include. To take counting words even further beyond the realm of possibility, we add an astonishing number of new words to our language every year. Bill Bryson, in *The Mother Tongue* (William Morrow, 1990), states that at the turn of the century, about 1,000 new words were added to English every year. As one might expect, with the rapid changes in technology and the world in general, the number of new words per year has grown exponentially, to an estimated 15,000 to 20,000 words per year. In 1987, when Random House updated its 1966 unabridged dictionary, it added 50,000 new words and 75,000 new definitions of old words. Two-thirds of the 315,000 entries from the 1966 edition had to be revised.

Explore

A. Go to the library or borrow the oldest dictionaries you can find. Look up the following words. At what point do they appear in the dictionary? Does one dictionary publisher seem to be quicker than others to include new words?

_____ preppy
_____ VCR
_____ quark
_____ sushi
_____ flextime
_____ crêpes
_____ chairperson
_____ tofu
_____ fax

At what point in time do the following definitions appear?

_____ web (as in World Wide Web)
_____ boot (as in boot up a computer)
_____ journal (as a verb)
_____ not! (slang)
_____ talk (to computers)
_____ log on

ECS Learning Systems, Inc.
The Grammar Notebook

B. Play "Stump the Dictionary." Try to think of words that have come into the language in the last 20 years that would not be in the older dictionaries or wouldn't have current meanings. (Hint: What kinds of technological or social changes have occurred in the last 20 years?)

ECS Learning Systems, Inc.

Capitalization

Capitalization Rules

First Words

1. Capitalize the first word of every sentence.

    Life is like a bowl of cherries.

    Give me liberty or give me death.

2. Capitalize the first word of a quotation, even if it's not a full sentence.

    Thomas Fuller said, "*All* rivers do what they can for the sea."

    Amy Fuller said, "*Really?*"

Names of People

1. Capitalize the names of people, including initials and titles of address.

    Babe Ruth   Mr. Brown   President Clinton   Sister Mary Rose

2. Capitalize words for family members if they are a part of a proper name. To test, use a real name in place of the word. If it makes sense, capitalize the family word.

    Wait, Mom.   Where's Grandma Louise?   She's with Sister.

3. Don't capitalize words for family members if they appear with a possessive pronoun or article. Again, to test, use a real name in place of the family word. If it doesn't make sense, don't capitalize the family word.

    my brother   her mom and dad   an uncle   our grandparents

4. Capitalize the pronoun *I*.

> Dad and *I* watched the Broncos.

> She's taller than *I* am.

5. Capitalize the names of religious icons.

> God   Allah   Jesus Christ

6. Capitalize the names of nationalities, races, peoples, and religions.

> American   Asian   Chicano   African   Jewish

7. Capitalize occupations only if they come before a proper noun.

> The *doctor* isn't in right now.

> Every week, *Pastor* Willems puts in long days.

Names of Places

1. Capitalize the names of countries, states, provinces, and cities.

> Panama   Colorado   British Columbia   Prague

2. Capitalize the names of oceans, lakes, rivers, islands, and mountains.

> the Pacific Ocean   Lake Erie   Mississippi River   Beaver Island   Pikes Peak

3. Capitalize the names of geographical areas.

> the West   the West Coast   the Southwest   the Rocky Mountains

4. Don't capitalize directions if they aren't names of geographical areas.

> We live west of the Mississippi.

> Go two blocks north, then a block east.

5. Capitalize names of schools, parks, buildings, and streets.

> Skyway Elementary   Memorial Park   Sears Tower   Cascade Avenue

     ECS Learning Systems, Inc.   The Grammar Notebook

Time Words

1. Capitalize names of days and months.

   Tuesday   March

2. Capitalize names of holidays and historical events.

   Christmas   Labor Day   the Battle of Little Big Horn

3. Don't capitalize names of seasons.

   spring   summer   fall   winter

   Exception: The names of seasons are capitalized only if they are used as **personifications**.

   Finally, *Summer* arrived in her radiant glory.

Titles

1. Capitalize the first word and all the important words in titles of books, magazines, newspapers, and articles. Do not capitalize short prepositions, conjunctions, or articles (*a, an, the*) if they come after the first word in the title.

   Gone with the Wind   *Newsweek*   *The Post*   "Living with Cancer"

2. Capitalize the first word and all the important words of names of movies, plays, radio programs, and television programs. Do not capitalize short prepositions, conjunctions, or articles (*a, an, the*) unless they are the first word in the title.

   "The Simpsons"   *Death of a Salesman*   *War and Peace*   *Star Wars*

Names of Organizations

1. Capitalize the names of organizations, government groups, and businesses.

   International Reading Association   the Senate   Starbucks

2. Capitalize trade names, but do not capitalize the name of the product.

   Apple computer   Ford truck   Adidas shoes

Other

1. Capitalize the names of languages.

   English   Spanish   Japanese

2. Don't capitalize school subjects unless they are the names of languages or are followed by a number.

   gym   algebra   German   Speech 101

      ECS Learning Systems, Inc.

It's Your Turn
Capitalization and Punctuation

I. **Directions:** On a separate sheet of paper, rewrite the following sentences, correcting the capitalization errors.

1. We sailed on the sea of Cortéz over Christmas Vacation last year.

2. Amy's Dad bought a new car this Summer, a Dodge Minivan.

3. Jess is taking english, spanish, algebra 201, Biology, and Band.

4. The class wanted french fries at their spanish fiesta.

5. The teacher said, "please read *tales from the crypt* for halloween."

6. The Principal at broadmoor elementary has swedish-design furniture.

7. The catholic church just West of us is having a good friday service.

8. Jayne's Stockbroker increased the value of her Gateway Computer stock portfolio by 20% this year.

9. Eli put up a Christmas Tree this year even though he's jewish.

10. My Uncle was elected to the Colorado senate this year.

II. **Directions:** Punctuate the following paragraphs. Remember to use capital letters at the beginning of each sentence.

my hair began to turn gray the year my boys Jess and Dusty turned four and two. jess took his job as older brother very seriously and constantly made helpful suggestions to Dusty who at half Jess' age only had half of his life experience wisdom and common sense. jess encouraged Dusty to swing from the living room curtains scale the refrigerator by way of the microwave and chug the tomato plants in the garden. the last item Jess announced as I was hosing down the kitchen after the boys had finished a spaghetti lunch Dusty and I chugged all the tomatoes for you, Mommy. I was quite pleased to discover that, already at four jess could conjugate the verb he had made up. when I asked him what chugged meant I was less thrilled to discover that chug meant yank out of the ground and throw in a pile. what was a mother to do.

ECS Learning Systems, Inc.

my friends with little girls casually shared that *their* little girls still took morning naps. *their* little girls loved to help fold laundry *their* little girls could sit quietly for hours with nothing more than a coloring book and a box of crayons which of course were all still wrapped in their papers. although my friends never said it I suspected that *they* suspected my boys were victims of sloppy free for all parenting. who knows? they may have been right. during those years it just didn't seem fair that my friends with girls had time to bake cookies and read magazines while I stayed buried under a laundry mountain of lunch-stained T shirts.

somewhere about the time our children started school though the tables began to shift. now my friends wailed my little girl comes home at least once a week in tears because this friend or that said she hates her. last week she cried for an hour because she was teased for having a purple lunch box instead of a pink one. girls can be so vicious having once been a young girl myself I would agree. being the mother of two boys means I rarely if ever, have to deal with tears and trauma. and I've certainly never had to comfort them over the color of a lunch box. I guess life has a way of evening things out. thank goodness

■ Write Your Own

Directions: On a separate sheet of paper, write sentences for the following prompts.

1. A quotation

2. Family words

3. Family word with a possessive pronoun

4. The name of a nationality, race, or religion

5. A place name

6. A list of the courses you are taking this year

7. The name of a magazine and the title of an article

8. The name of an organization or government group

9. Your favorite holiday and the season in which it falls

10. The name of the vehicle you would like to buy

ECS Learning Systems, Inc.   The Grammar Notebook

Review

■ What Have You Learned So Far?

Reflect back on your learning process so far. What has been easy to learn? What has been difficult? What in the text helps you to learn? What can you do to improve how you're learning? Think about these questions as you answer the following:

1. What have you learned about punctuation and mechanics?

2. How has this changed your use of language?

3. What are you still not sure about? How will you gain clarification?

4. What additional information do you want to learn about punctuation and mechanics?

ECS Learning Systems, Inc.

Spelling

Commonly Confused Words

Which is Which?

Many words that sound alike or have similar spellings are misused so often that their meanings have become confused. Even experienced writers occasionally confuse certain words—at least in their rough drafts. Good writers know which words cause them problems. As they proofread, they keep a careful watch for those words.

Most of the time writers use simple **mnemonic devices** (memory techniques) to help remember which words to use when. The easiest way to remember is to substitute a *synonym* (a word with a similar meaning) or another word that is the same part of speech for the word in question. If in doubt, though, look it up.

Accept/Except

Accept is a verb meaning "to receive" (usually favorably). *Except* is usually a preposition. *Except* can also be a verb meaning "to exclude."

> **Verb and Preposition:** She *accepted* congratulations from everyone *except* her opponent.

> **Verb:** She will *except* her opponent from the guest list.

Affect/Effect

Affect is usually a verb meaning "to influence." *Effect* is usually a noun meaning "result."

> **Verb:** The medicine *affected* him in a negative way.

> **Noun:** He didn't like the *effect* of the medicine.

All ready/Already

All ready means "completely prepared." *Already* means "before."

> **Prepared:** Dinner is *all ready*.

> **Before:** Unfortunately, Dad has *already* eaten.

　　ECS Learning Systems, Inc.

All Right

All right means "satisfactory." It is always written as two words. *Alright* is the nonstandard spelling and is not appropriate unless used intentionally.

All together/Altogether

All together means "everyone" or "everything gathered." *Altogether* means "entirely" or "completely."

> **Everyone:** We spent the week ***all together***.

> **Entirely:** This is ***altogether*** too much work.

A lot/Alot

A lot means "a great deal." It is always written as two words. *Alot* is the nonstandard spelling of *a lot* and is not appropriate.

Anyways/Anywheres

Both *anyways* and *anywheres* are nonstandard. Instead, use *anyway* and *anywhere*.

A while/Awhile

Awhile is an adverb. As such, it never follows a preposition such as *for*. Only nouns can be the objects of a preposition. *A while* is an article and noun. Both can follow a preposition.

> **Adverb:** Stay ***awhile***.

> **Article and noun:** Stay for ***a while***.

Bad/Badly

Bad is an adjective. *Badly* is an adverb.

> **Adjective:** It was a ***bad*** day when she ran over the cat.

> **Adverb:** Fortunately, the cat was not ***badly*** hurt.

Beside/Besides

Both *beside* and *besides* are prepositions. *Beside* means "at the side of" or "next to." *Besides* means "except" or "in addition to."

> **Next to:** I sat *beside* my husband.

> **Except:** No one volunteered *besides* me.

Bring/Take

Use *bring* when something is being carried *to* a person, place, or thing. Use *take* when it is being carried *away from* the person, place, or thing.

> **To:** Mrs. Travis is *bringing* a blackberry pie to the potluck.

> **From:** She won't have any pie left to *take* home.

Can/May

Can is used in reference to ability. *May* refers to permission.

> **Ability:** Ellen *can* swim across the lake.

> **Permission:** She *may* not do it unless a lifeguard is on duty.

Capital/Capitol

Capital refers either to a city or to wealth or resources. *Capitol* refers to a government building.

> **City:** Denver is the *capital* of Colorado.

> **Building:** The *capitol* has a gold dome.

Cite/Site/Sight

Cite means "to quote or refer to another source." *Site* means "a location." *Sight* refers to "seeing."

> **Quote:** She *cites* Shakespeare every chance she gets.

> **Location:** Steve is working on the construction *site* today.

> **Seeing:** He was a *sight* for sore eyes.

Complement/Compliment

Both *complement* and *compliment* can either be verbs or nouns. *Complement* means "an addition to" or "to add to" or "to complete." *Compliment* means "praise" or "to praise."

Complete: A matching hat *complemented* her outfit.

Praise: He *complimented* her on her outfit.

Continual/Continuous

Continual means "frequently repeated." *Continuous* means "without any stops."

Repeated: The child's *continual* whining irritated everyone.

No stopping: The *continuous* buzzing of the light bulb was annoying.

Could Care Less

"Could care less" is an inaccurate expression. The accurate expression is "*couldn't* care less." If someone *could* care less, it means he or she still cares somewhat.

etc.

In formal writing, avoid using *etc*. It's better to end with an actual example or the phrase "and so on."

Every one/Everyone

Everyone means "every single person." *Every one* is usually followed by the word *of* and means "each one."

All: *Everyone* sang along.

Each one: *Every one* of the students sang along.

Farther/Further

Farther refers to physical distance. *Further* refers to degree or quantity.

Distance: We traveled *farther* than we thought we would.

Degree: We've come *further* in life than we expected.

Fewer/Less

Use *fewer* for things that can be counted. Use *less* for items that can't be counted.

Countable: The school library has *fewer* books than the public library.

Not countable: I have *less* courage than I thought I did.

Get

Get is often used inappropriately as a substitute for the word *go*.

Awkward: I have to *get* to work.

Better: I have to *go* to work.

Good/Well

Good is an adjective. *Well* is an adverb. *Well* can also describe a state of health.

Adjective: Mary is a *good* driver.

Adverb: She drives *well* on ice and snow.

Health: After being sick for three days, it's nice to feel *well* again.

Hopefully

Hopefully means "in a hopeful manner." Many grammarians would say that it's incorrect to use *hopefully* to mean "it is to be hoped that" because it is an adverb that must modify another word. In reality, many adverbs function in this way. It is considered better grammar, though, to substitute *hopefully* with *I hope*.

Imply/Infer

Imply means "to suggest something indirectly." *Infer* means "to draw a conclusion from what has been said."

Suggestion: He *implied* that he would show up at 9:00 a.m.

Conclusion: We *inferred* that he would probably be late.

ECS Learning Systems, Inc.

Irregardless:

Irregardless is nonstandard usage and is not appropriate in speech or writing. Use *regardless* instead.

It's/Its

It's is a contraction for "it is." *Its* is a possessive pronoun.

> **It is:** *It's* getting late.

> **Possessive:** This is *its* home.

Know/No:

Know means "to recognize" or "to understand." *No* is the opposite of *yes*.

> **Recognize:** I *know* most of my neighbors.

> **Opposite of yes:** *No,* you may not stay up late.

Leave/Let

Leave means "to go away." *Let* means "to allow."

> **Go away:** *Leave* the room.

> **Allow:** *Let* me do it myself.

Lie/Lay

Lie is the present tense form of the verb meaning "to recline." *Lay* is the present tense form of the verb meaning "to put or place." *Lay* is also the simple past tense form of *lie*. *Lie* is also a verb or noun meaning "to tell an untruth."

> **Recline (present):** I *lie* down every day for a nap.

> **Recline (past):** Yesterday, I *lay* down for only 15 minutes.

> **Put or place:** *Lay* the magazines on the coffee table when you're finished reading.

> **Tell an untruth:** Did you *lie* about eating all the cookies?

Loose/Lose

Loose means "not fastened or restrained." *Lose* is a verb meaning "to be unable to find."

> **Not fastened:** Wear *loose* clothes for hiking.

> **Unable to find:** Don't *lose* your keys.

Maybe/May be

Maybe is an adverb meaning "possibly." *May be* is a verb phrase.

> **Possibly:** *Maybe* I'll get out of class early.

> **Verb Phrase:** We *may be* let out of class early.

Moral/Morale/Morel

Moral refers to rules or habits of conduct. *Morale* refers to the spiritual state of an individual or a group. *Morel* is a kind of mushroom.

> **Rule of conduct:** Most fables have a *moral* lesson.

> **State of spirit:** The win gave the team's *morale* a boost.

> **Mushroom:** The ground was covered with *morels*.

Of/Have

Have should be used instead of the preposition *of* after the verbs *could, would, should, might, must,* and *may*. Using *of* instead of *have* is nonstandard and inappropriate in speech and writing.

> **Nonstandard:** She *would of* worked all night.

> **Standard:** She *would have* worked all night.

Our/Are

Our is a possessive pronoun. *Are* is a verb.

> **Possessive:** This is *our* house.

> **Verb:** They *are* here.

Passed/Past

Passed is the past tense of the verb *pass*. *Past* is a noun or an adjective referring to "something that belongs to an earlier time."

> **Verb:** He *passed* the test.

> **Earlier time:** The *past* year has been a good one.

Principal/Principle

A *principal* is a person or a sum of money. It can also be an adjective meaning "the most important." *Principle* is also a noun meaning "an ethic or a basic truth or law."

> **Person:** The *principal* hired a new teacher.

> **Sum of Money:** The *principal* on my car loan is $5000.

> **Adjective:** The *principal* reason she hired him is because he's her son.

> **Truth:** A *principle* of life is that life isn't fair.

Quiet/Quite

Quiet means "silent or calm." *Quite* means "very."

> **Silent:** The baby is finally *quiet*.

> **Very:** The new lawyer is *quite* sure of herself.

Real/Really

Real is an adjective; *really* is an adverb. In informal English, people sometimes use *real* as either an adjective or adverb; however, this is nonstandard.

> **Adjective:** The plate is *real* bone china.

> **Adverb:** I'm *really* (not *real*) tired.

Right/Rite/Write

Right means "correct" or "the opposite of left." *Rite* means "ritual." *Write* means "to put something on paper."

Opposite of left: Take a *right* at the next intersection.

Ritual: Shaving is a *rite* of passage for most boys.

Put on paper: My mother *writes* every week.

Set/Sit

Set means "to place" or "to put something." It takes an object. *Sit* means "to be seated."

Put or place: *Set* the book on the table.

Be seated: *Sit* down.

Stationary/Stationery

Stationary means "not moving." *Stationery* is writing paper.

Not moving: She rides a *stationary* bike while she watches TV.

Writing paper: She bought flowered *stationery*.

Sometime/Sometimes/Some time

Sometime and *sometimes* are adverbs. *Sometime* means "at an unstated time." *Sometimes* means "at times." *Some time* is an adjective and noun, with *some* describing the noun *time*. It means "a period of time."

Unstated time: We'll leave *sometime* tomorrow.

At times: *Sometimes* the light switch doesn't work.

Period of time: I have *some time* to help you.

Than/Then

Than is used for comparisons. *Then* is an adverb that refers to time.

Comparison: Milk is better for you *than* pop.

Time: We'll stop by the office, *then* grab a bite to eat.

ECS Learning Systems, Inc.

Their/There/They're

Their is a possessive pronoun. *There* refers to a place or position. *They're* is a contraction for *they are*.

> **Possessive:** *Their* car is parked illegally.

> **Place:** Put the groceries over *there*.

> **They are:** *They're* coming for lunch on Friday.

Through/Threw/Thorough

Through is a preposition meaning "by means of" or "into" or "out of." *Threw* is the past tense of the verb *throw*. *Thorough* is an adjective meaning "careful" or "complete."

> **Preposition:** Alice stepped *through* the looking glass.

> **Verb:** Molly *threw* a tantrum.

> **Adjective:** The detective did a *thorough* check of the room.

To/Too/Two

To is a preposition that means "toward." It can also be the first word of an infinitive phrase. *Too* is an adverb that means "very" or "also." *Two* is the number 2.

> **Preposition:** The dog ran *to* the end of the drive.

> **Very:** It's *too* cold for swimming.

> **Number:** We have *two* sons.

Waist/Waste

The *waist* is "the middle part of the body." *Waste* is trash. *Waste* can also be a verb meaning "to squander" or a noun meaning "something squandered."

> **Body:** His father's belt was too large for his *waist*.

> **Something squandered:** Letting these tomatoes rot would be a *waste*.

ECS Learning Systems, Inc.   The Grammar Notebook

Weather/Whether

Weather refers to climate. *Whether* is a conjunction that introduces alternatives.

Climate: We usually have hot *weather* in August.

Conjunction: They can't decide *whether* to go on vacation or paint the house.

Who's/Whose

Who's is a contraction for "who is." *Whose* is a possessive pronoun.

Who is: *Who's* coming for dinner?

Possessive pronoun: *Whose* jacket is on the floor?

Your/You're

Your is a possessive pronoun. *You're* is a contraction of *you are*.

Possessive pronoun: *Your* understanding of grammar is improving!

You are: *You're* becoming an expert.

■ Discuss

Alot and *alright* are commonly used, even though they are nonstandard. Will they eventually become standard? Will their meanings be slightly different from their two-word counterparts? Think about the subtle differences of *all together* and *altogether* or *all ready* and *already*. If English teachers finally give up the fight, what subtle distinction might there be between *all right* and *alright*? Between *a lot* and *alot*?

ECS Learning Systems, Inc.

It's Your Turn
Commonly Confused Words

Directions: Cross out the incorrect words in the following sentences. Write the correct word below the incorrect word.

~~Irregardless~~ of whose fault this is, ~~your~~ going to clean up the mess.
  Regardless   **you're**

1. Its going to be to hot too be comfortable today.

2. Their won't be any way to cool off accept to go swimming.

3. Alot of the kids in the neighborhood have all ready decided too go to the pool.

4. Their planning a big party too celebrate the end of summer.

5. Its all together possible that it will last passed midnight.

6. Every one is assigned a food too take.

7. They're could of been a problem with this.

8. But the mom whose in charge of the planning has done this alot.

9. She's all ways through and real careful about who takes what.

10. Its certainly alright with everyone that she takes on the responsibility.

■ Write Your Own

Choose five sets of words from the previous pages (or from your own set of words) that are most difficult for you to remember. On a separate sheet of paper, write two sentences for each of the words you have trouble with. What are some tricks you can use to remember when to use which word?

Spelling Visualization Strategy

Spelling is a writing skill. Most of us can understand, say, and read many words we can't spell. To improve your spelling, improve your visualization skills. In most cases, it is much easier to picture a word and then write it than to sound out a word and write it.

Practice the following steps as you learn to spell a new word or a troublesome old one. An important key to learning how to spell a word is to make sure you know what the word means and how it's used.

1. Write the word on a note card. Hold the card so you have to look up to see the word.

2. Using your eye as a pencil, trace each letter in the word. Note and remember which letters go up or down. How many vowels are there? In what order are they? Are there any silent letters? Double letters? Small words within the word? What trouble spots do you have? Put those letters in red in your mind or put a box around them. Play with the letters in this way until you have a clear visual memory of the word.

3. Put the card down and look up again. Can you "see" the word? (If you can't, repeat step 2 until you can.) Again, play with the word. Ask yourself questions: What letters go up or down? What are the vowels? What words are within the word?

4. When you feel confident that you have a good visual memory of the word, spell the word forward, then backward. "Look" at the letters as you spell. Don't use your ear or memory, just your eyes. When you can spell the word backward as quickly as you can spell it forward, you know the word.

5. Again, hold up the note card with the word on it. Take a mental picture of it.

6. Write the word on your paper without looking at the card. Be conscious of how the word feels as you write it. When does your hand go up or down? Pay attention to how your body reacts: If your brow wrinkles at a point in the word, or if your hand pulls back, you've probably written a wrong letter. Go back and fix the word.

7. Look at the word one last time. Does it match what you've written? If not, go back and fix your visual memory of the word. Exaggerate the problem spots: Put them in red in your mind, or put them in a box. Recognize these as trouble spots, and be aware of them when you spell the word.

ECS Learning Systems, Inc.

Spelling Rules

In spite of the unpredictability of English spelling, some standard rules apply. Use the Spelling Visualization Strategy to help you memorize the following rules and their exceptions.

Rule 1: *i* before *e*

Put *i* before *e*,
except after *c*,
or when sounded like *a*,
as in *neighbor* or *weigh*.

i before *e*	except after *c*	sounds like *a*
achieve	conceit	deign
believe	conceive	eight
fiend	ceiling	freight
fierce	deceit	neighbor
grief	deceive	reign
relieve	perceive	skein
reprieve	receipt	vein
retrieve	receive	weigh
sieve		

Some Exceptions

Which of the following exceptions to the rule are difficult to remember? Look for patterns or mnemonic strategies to help you remember the exceptions. For instance, several of the exceptions contain the letter combination *cien*.

ancient	counterfeit	foreign	heifer	proficient
caffeine	deficient	forfeit	height	protein
codeine	efficient	financier	leisure	seize
conscience	either	glacier	neither	weird

■ Write Your Own

Directions: Choose five words from the list or that are exceptions to the *i* before *e* rule. On a separate sheet of paper, write two sentences for each. What are some tricks you can use to remember the correct spelling of words that have *i* and *e*?

ECS Learning Systems, Inc.   The Grammar Notebook

Rule 2: Prefixes

A root word does not change its spelling when a prefix is added to it.

Prefix	+ Root	= New Word
a-	moral	amoral
ab-	normal	abnormal
dis-	satisfied	dissatisfied
e-	migrate	emigrate
im-	pure	impure
in-	conspicuous	inconspicuous
mis-	spell	misspell
un-	necessary	unnecessary

When two words are combined into a single word, it becomes a *compound word*. Both words retain their original spellings.

Word	+ Word	= Compound Word
book	mark	bookmark
life	line	lifeline
proof	read	proofread
push	over	pushover
out	wit	outwit
town	house	townhouse

Some Exceptions

Some commonly used compounds have dropped letters. Because they're exceptions to the rule, they're often misspelled. Notice that when *all* or *full* is part of the compound, one *l* is usually dropped.

almost	fulfill	useful
already	fulfillment	welcome
always	meaningful	wherever
artful	pastime	

■ Write Your Own

Directions: Choose five words you have trouble with or that are exceptions to the prefix or compound rules. On a separate sheet of paper, write two sentences for each. What are some tricks you can use to remember how to spell compound words or words with prefixes?

ECS Learning Systems, Inc.

Rule 3: Suffixes–Silent *e*

If a word ends with a silent *e*, DROP the *e* before adding a suffix that begins with a vowel.

-ing, -ed	*-able*	*-ation*	*-ive*
amusing	adorable	adoration	abusive
believed	believable	continuation	creative
enduring	endurable	declaration	decorative
hoped	excitable	duration	expensive
loving	lovable	motivation	intensive
pleased	pleasurable	quotation	repulsive

If a word ends with a silent *e*, DO NOT drop the silent *e* if the suffix begins with a consonant.

-ful	*-ment*	*-ly*	*-ness*
careful	achievement	closely	crudeness
disgraceful	acknowledgement	extremely	genuineness
hopeful	excitement	lately	likeness
spiteful	improvement	lively	rudeness
suspenseful	management	timely	sameness
wasteful	placement	widely	wideness

Some Exceptions

Some of the following words are exceptions to keeping the final *e*, and some are exceptions to dropping the final *e*. Note that when a suffix begins with the letter *a* or when the letter *o* is added to a word that ends in *-ce* or *-ge*, DO NOT drop the final *e*.

acreage	courageous	judgment	replaceable
advantageous	duly	manageable	serviceable
argument	duty	noticeable	truly
awful	dyeing	outrageous	
changeable	exchanging	peaceable	

■ Write Your Own

Directions: Choose five words that follow or are exceptions to this suffix rule. On a separate sheet of paper, write two sentences for each. What are some tricks you can use to remember how to spell these words?

Rule 4: Suffixes –y

If a word ends with a *y*, CHANGE the *y* to *i* before adding a suffix unless the suffix begins with the letter *i*.

-er, -est, -ly, -ness	*-ous*	*-ance, -ant*	*-able, -ful*
craftier	industrious	alliance	beautiful
healthiest	luxurious	compliant	bountiful
heavily	mysterious	defiance	justifiable
holiness	studious	reliant	merciful

If a word ends with a *y*, DO NOT CHANGE or drop the *y* if it is preceded by another vowel or if the suffix begins with *i*.

babying	flying	partying
complying	lying	supplying
crying	marrying	trying

Some Exceptions

-ly, -ness	*-ous*	*others*
dryly	beauteous	daily
dryness	bounteous	gaily
shyly	miscellaneous	
shyness		
slyly		
slyness		

■ Write Your Own

Directions: Choose five words that follow or that are exceptions to this suffix rule. On a separate sheet of paper, write two sentences for each. What are some tricks you can use to remember how to spell these words?

ECS Learning Systems, Inc.

Rule 5: Suffixes –*ly*

When -*ly* is added to a word, the spelling of the base word usually doesn't change.

absently	expectantly	likely	quickly
definitely	graciously	poorly	slowly

Exceptions

When -*ly* is added to a word ending with -*le*, drop the -*le* and replace it with -*ly*.

forcibly	probably	terribly
illegibly	suitably	

When the base word ends with a *y* following a consonant, the *y* is changed to *i* before -*ly*.

busily	heavily	merrily
daintily	lazily	sleepily
happily	luckily	testily

■ Write Your Own

Directions: Choose five words that follow or are exceptions to this suffix rule. On a separate sheet of paper, write two sentences for each. What are some tricks you can use to remember how to spell these words?

ECS Learning Systems, Inc.   The Grammar Notebook

Rule 6: Suffixes–Single Syllables

If a one-syllable word ends in a single consonant preceded by a single vowel, DOUBLE the final consonant when adding a suffix that begins with a vowel. Follow this rule for words with more than one syllable if the accent is on the last syllable.

single vowel, single consonant	-ed, -er, -ing
bed	bedding
commit	committed, committing
defer	deferred, deferring
dig	digger, digging
get	getting
hit	hitter, hitting
infer	inferred, inferring
occur	occurred, occurring
peg	pegged, pegging
permit	permitted, permitting
prefer	preferred, preferring
propel	propelled, propeller
submit	submitted, submitting
step	stepped, stepping
win	winner, winning
wrap	wrapped, wrapped, wrapping

Some Exceptions

In one-syllable words that end in *x* preceded by a single vowel, DO NOT double the *x*.

box	boxes, boxer, boxed
fax	faxes, faxing, faxed
fox	foxes

ECS Learning Systems, Inc.

If a word ends in two consonants or two vowels and a consonant, DO NOT double the final consonant when adding a suffix that begins with a vowel. Follow this rule also for words with more than one syllable if the accent is on the last syllable.

two consonants, two vowels and a consonant	-ed, -er, -ing
green	greener, greening
contain	container, containing
detour	detoured, detouring
exceed	exceeded, exceeding
flood	flooded, flooding
form	formed, former
pump	pumped, pumping
quick	quicker
read	reader, reading
regard	regarded, regarding
tear	tearing

Some Exceptions

Treat *qu* as a consonant rather than a consonant and a vowel.

equip	equipped, equipping
quip	quipped, quipping
quit	quitter, quitting
quiz	quizzes, quizzing

■ Write Your Own

Directions: Choose five words that follow or that are exceptions to this suffix rule. On a separate sheet of paper, write two sentences for each. What are some tricks you can use to remember how to spell these words?

ECS Learning Systems, Inc.   The Grammar Notebook

Rule 7: Suffixes–Two or More Syllables

If a word with two or more syllables ends with a vowel and one consonant, follow Rule 6 if the accent is on the last syllable.

single vowel, single consonant	-ed, -er, -ing, -ance, -at, etc.
acquit	acquittal
admit	admittance
befit	befitting
disbar	disbarred
excel	excellence
occur	occurrence
transmit	transmittal

If a word with two or more syllables ends with a vowel and one consonant, DO NOT double the final consonant if the accent is not on the last syllable or the suffix begins with a consonant.

single vowel, single consonant	-ed, -er, -ing, -ance, -at, -ment, -ence, -er accent not on final syllable
benefit	benefited
blossom	blossomed
bullet	bulleted
commit	commitment
defer	deferment
differ	differed, difference
equip	equipment
profit	profited, profiting
quarrel	quarreling
retain	retained, retainer
solicit	solicited
summon	summoned

■ Write Your Own

I. **Directions:** Choose five words that follow or are exceptions to this suffix rule. On a separate sheet of paper, write two sentences for each. What are some tricks you can use to remember how to spell these words?

II. **Directions:** On a separate sheet of paper, write the correct spelling for as many variations on the following words as you can think of. Identify the rule (or the exception to the rule) for each one you have trouble with.

base	-er, -ed, -ing, -ment, -ly, -ful, -able, -ness, -y, etc.
1. acquit	acquitted, acquitting, acquittal
2. commit	
3. content	
4. develop	
5. equip	
6. heavy	
7. like	
8. quiet	
9. solicit	
10. benefit	
11. occur	
12. quiz	
13. exceed	
14. definite	
15. craft	
16. healthy	
17. mercy	
18. necessary	
19. satisfy	
20. permanent	

Spelling Demons

Some words do not follow the rules. For instance, *analysis* and *analyze* must simply be memorized: No rule will tell you when to use the letter **s** and when to use the letter **z**. Many demons result from the difference between common English pronunciation and how a word evolved. Some difficulties arise because letters have dropped out of a word. Examples of this are words like *always*, *pastime*, or *judgment*.

Highlight the words in the following list that are troublesome for you. To help you learn them, use the strategies listed below.

- Use the Visualization Strategy to build a strong mental picture of the word.

- Group like words together.

- Create mnemonic devices to help you remember (*Atten**dance** at the **dance** was good.*).

- Practice writing the words correctly.

A
aberration
abscess
absence
abundance
acceptable
accessible
accidentally
accommodate
accumulation
accuracy
accustomed
achieve
acknowledge
acquaintance
acquire
across
actually
address
adequately
adjunct
admittance
adolescence

advertise
advice
affected
affectionately
against
aggravate
aggressive
a lot
alleged
all right
allotted
almost
already
always
although
altogether
amateur
amendment
among
analysis
analyze
ancient
anecdote

annihilate
announcement
annoyance
annual
answer
apparatus
apparent
appearance
appreciate
approximately
arctic
argument
arising
arithmetic
arraignment
arrangement
arrest
ascend
ascertain
assassination
assessment
association

atheist
athlete

B
basically
bazaar
beginning
beleaguered
belief
believe
beneficial
benefited
benefiting
bizarre
breath
breathe
brilliant
Britain
bureau
bureaucracy
busily
business

ECS Learning Systems, Inc.

C

cafeteria
caffeine
calculator
calendar
calf, calves
candidate
category
ceiling
cemetery
certainly
changeable
character
chief
chocolate
choose
chosen
codeine
column
coming
commercial
commission
commitment
committal
committed
committee
community
compatible
competent
competition
competitive
completely
conceivable
concentrate
condemn
confectionery
conferred
confidence
conqueror
conscience
conscientious
conscious
consistent
continuous
controlled
controversial
convenience
convenient
correlation
counselor
counterfeit
courageous
courteous
courtesy
cousin
criticism
criticize
cruelty
crystallized
curiosity
curious
currency

D

dealt
deceive
decide
decision
defendant
deferred
deficient
definitely
dependent
derogatory
descendant
describe
description
desecrated
despair
desperate
develop
dictionary
difference
different
dilapidated
dilemma
dining
disagree
disappearance
disappoint
disapprove
disastrous
disciple
discipline
discussion
disease
dissatisfied
distinguish
divide
doctor
dormitory

E

ecstasy
efficiency
efficient
eighth
either
elaborately
eligible
eliminate
embarrass
eminent
emphasize
emphatically
enough
enthusiasm
entirely
entrance
environment
equivalent
especially
essential
evidently
exaggerate
exceed
excellent
excitement
exercise
exhaust
exhortation
existence
explanation
extraordinary
extremely

F

familiar
fascinate
favorite
February
feudal
finally
financially
financier
foreign
foresee
forfeit
forty
forward
fourth
friend
fulfill

G

gaiety
gaudy
gauge
genius
generally
glacier
government
governor
grammar
grief
guarantee
guard
guidance

H

half
halves
happily
harassment
heifer
height
heir
heritage
heroes
hindrance
hoping
humorous

ECS Learning Systems, Inc. The Grammar Notebook

hungry
hypocrisy
hypocrite

I

ideally
ignorant
illogical
illiterate
imaginary
imagination
imagine
imitation
immediately
immense
imminent
impartiality
incense
incidentally
incongruous
incredible
indefinitely
independent
indict
independent
indispensable
inevitable
infinite
influential
initiate
innocuous
insistent
intelligence
interest
interpret
interrupt
irascible
irrelevant
irreparable
irresistible
irritated

J

jeopardy
journal

joyous
judgment

K

knives
knowledge

L

laboratory
lacquer
lavender
league
legitimate
leisure
length
library
license
lightning
likelihood
liquid
literature
loneliness
loose
lose
lying

M

magazine
magnificence
maintenance
manageable
maneuver
marriage
marriageable
masquerade
mathematics
matinee
meant
mechanical
medicine
memoir
miniature
minutes
mischievous

missile
mortgage
muscle
mysterious

N

necessary
negligible
neither
nickel
niece
ninety
ninth
noticeable
noticing
nuclear
nuisance
numerous

O

obstacle
occasion
occasionally
occur
occurred
occurrence
official
omission
omitted
opponent
opportunity
opposite
optimism
optimistic
originally
outrageous

P

paid
pamphlet
panicky
parallel
paralleled
parliamentary
particularly
pastime

patient
peaceable
peculiar
perceive
performance
persistent
permanent
permissible
perseverance
persistence
personnel
perspiration
phenomenon
phony
physical
picnicking
planning
pleasant
pneumonia
poison
politician
possession
possibly
possession
potatoes
primitive
privilege
probably
procedure
proceed
professor
proficient
prominent
pronunciation
protein
psychology
publicity
punctilious
purpose
pursing
pursue

Q

quantity
questionnaire

ECS Learning Systems, Inc.

quiet
quite
quizzes

R

realistically
realize
receipt
receive
recognize
recommend
reference
referred
referring
regard
regrettable
reign
rehearsal
relevant
religion
religious
remembrance
reminisce
repetition
repetitious
resemblance
resilience
restaurant
rhetorical
rhythm
rhythmical
ridiculous
roommate

S

sacrilegious
safety
sandwich
scarcity
schedule
science
scissors
secretary
seize
self
selves

separate
sergeant
several
shelf
shelves
sheriff
shining
siege
significance
similar
sincerely
skiing
soliloquy
sophomore
source
sovereign
specialty
specialized
specifically
specimen
speech
sponsor
staunch
stopping
straight
strength
strenuous
strict
strictly
stubbornness
studying
subtle
subtly
subversive
succeed
successful
succession
sufficient
summary
superintendent
supersede
suppress
surely
surgeon
surprise

susceptible
suspicious
symmetrical

T

technical
technique
temperature
tendency
than
their
then
theory
therefore
thief
thieves
thorough
through
together
tomorrow
tongue
tragedy
transferred
transient
tremendous
tries
truly
Tuesday
twelfth
tyranny

U

unanimous
unconscious
undoubtedly
unnecessarily
unnecessary
until
usage
usually

V

vacillate
vacuum
valuable
various

vegetable
vengeance
vicious
villain
violence
visible

W

weather
Wednesday
weird
wherever
whether
wholly
wield
wives
woman
women
worshiped
writing
written

Y

yacht
yield

ECS Learning Systems, Inc.   The Grammar Notebook

Language Play: Dictionaries

The first English language dictionary, *Cawdrey's Table Alphabeticall*, was published in 1604. A mere 100 pages, it contained only 3,000 words, not all of them even correctly spelled or alphabetized (check out that extra "**l**" in the title).

One hundred fifty years later, Samuel Johnson's dictionary arrived on the scene. It, too, was less than perfect: He perpetuated many inconsistencies in spelling (such as *downhil* and *uphill*, *hark* and *hearken*, and *deceit* and *receipt*), allowed some peculiar contradictions (*leeward* and *windward* share the same definition), and had an affinity for long-winded sentences (many ran 250 words or more). In spite of these flaws, his nine-year effort produced a remarkable benchmark for all dictionaries to come. His 43,000 words are concisely defined and accurate.

Seventy years later, in 1828, Noah Webster produced the definitive dictionary on this side of the Atlantic. In spite of some glaring flaws (he allowed ungrammatical usages, such as "we was" and "them horses"; he also fiddled with spelling—*groop/group*, *croud/crowd*, *medicin/medicine*), his 70,000 words were models of clarity and conciseness. The dictionary not only became the standard authority for the time, but it is still published today under the name Merriam-Webster (after the G.C. Merriam Company bought the rights and cleaned up Webster's more outlandish spellings and other errors).

The last milestone in dictionaries came with the publication of the *Unabridged Oxford English Dictionary*, which took 49 years to write and contained 414,825 entries. The 13-volume work appeared in stages, with *A to Ant* being published in 1884 and the last volume in 1928. This momentous achievement claimed to include every word in the language (aside from obscenities). In 1989, a second, updated version was published. This one included 615,000 entries and 2,412,000 supporting quotations.

A characteristic of the early dictionaries was the attempt to make the work **prescriptive** rather than **descriptive**. A prescriptive dictionary prescribes, or sets the standards for, language use. A descriptive dictionary describes, without adding a judgment, how language is used. Today, both kinds of dictionaries can be found.

ECS Learning Systems, Inc.

Explore

A. Look up the following words. From the citations given, do you think your dictionary is prescriptive or descriptive? (All of the questions are about usage unless otherwise noted.)

	Prescriptive	Descriptive
ain't	_____	_____
alright	_____	_____

	Prescriptive	Descriptive
alot	_____	_____
anyways	_____	_____
anywheres	_____	_____
can and may	_____	_____
imply and infer	_____	_____
flout and flaunt	_____	_____
disinterested and uninterested	_____	_____
lay	_____	_____
irregardless	_____	_____
February (pronunciation)	_____	_____

If a word is not included, would that suggest that the dictionary is prescriptive or descriptive?

B. How effectively does a dictionary that is *prescriptive*, rather than *descriptive*, affect language? Can a dictionary *affect* language usage? What impact would dictionaries have if they were only descriptive? What should be the final source in language usage? Should there even be one? Who or what should determine whether a usage is informal, formal, standard, or nonstandard? Who or what determines this?

ECS Learning Systems, Inc.   The Grammar Notebook

Review

■ What Have You Learned So Far?

Reflect back on your learning process so far. What has been easy to learn? What has been difficult? What in the text helps you to learn? What can you do to improve how you're learning? Think about these questions as you answer the following:

1. What have you learned about usage and spelling?

2. How has this changed your use of language?

3. What are you still not sure about? How will you gain clarification?

4. What additional information do you want to learn about usage and spelling?

ECS Learning Systems, Inc.

Appendix

Teaching What You Know

One of the most effective ways to learn something is to teach it. Use the following to plan what and how you'll teach.

1. What concept will you teach? It's not necessary to choose something you understand thoroughly. In fact, for the purpose of this exercise, you may want to choose a concept that you find difficult or confusing. In the process of preparing to teach, you'll be more likely to look at the concept from another perspective and explain it in a new way.

2. To whom will you teach it? What does this person or group already know about this concept? Do they consider it an easy or difficult concept?

3. In what ways is this concept similar to something your audience already knows well?

4. In what ways does the concept fit or break the rules your audience knows?

5. What strategies can you give your audience to help them to learn and remember the concept?

6. How can you combine visual, auditory, and kinesthetic elements into the lesson? How will you reinforce the learning?

ECS Learning Systems, Inc.   The Grammar Notebook

What's Your Learning Style?

Traditionally, most school subjects are taught with the teacher doing all the talking and the students doing all the listening. Some students are able to learn easily this way, but most learn best by using one or a combination of sensory learning styles: **Visual**—watching or reading, **Auditory**—listening, or **Kinesthetic**—touching or doing. Learning efficiency improves when all three styles are used together.

To help determine your own learning style, highlight or underline the following characteristics that describe how you most like to learn.

Visual	Auditory	Kinesthetic
prefer to watch first then do	prefer to have instructions given verbally	prefer to learn by doing
stay focused on the task	easily distracted	like to be in motion
notice detail	enjoy listening to books on tape	use hands while talking
careful about appearance	hum or sigh, often without realizing it	dress for comfort
good speller	poor speller	poor speller
remember faces	sometimes have trouble with written instructions	touch people while talking
quiet by nature	outgoing by nature	outgoing, often very expressive
good handwriting	enjoy talking	like to try new things
organized, like things in neat piles	distracted by noises	like activities
good at puzzles	like rhythm	enjoy dramas
enjoy reading	like to be read to	have low interest in reading
memorize by seeing	memorize by hearing	memorize by doing

New Word List

Word_____

How you learned it

_____

_____

_____

How and when you used it

_____

_____

_____

Word_____

How you learned it

_____

_____

_____

How and when you used it

_____

_____

_____

ECS Learning Systems, Inc.   The Grammar Notebook

Usage Errors

Error

_____

_____

_____

_____

What the correct usage should be

_____

_____

_____

_____

Was the error intentional? _____

What impact does the error have on the reader or listener?

_____

_____

_____

_____

The Grammar Notebook   ECS Learning Systems, Inc.

Answer Key

5 Commas

1. Lisa's husband, Brent, is a good attorney, isn't he?
2. "No one," Eleanor Roosevelt once said, "can make you feel inferior without your consent."
3. On the other hand, Mary would like to get the family together on July 3 instead of July 4.
4. The scientists, known for studying insects, were able to watch their behavior in close detail.
5. Sam left for London, England, with his best friend, Ellen.
6. The kids built a really elaborate treehouse in the back yard and decorated it with colored lights for Christmas.
7. March 15, 1994, was the last time we had more than two feet of snow from one storm.
8. In June 1996 the Bartels vacationed at the Grand Canyon, hiked two mountains, and had a family reunion.
9. Of all the books I read this summer, I enjoyed *Stormy Weather*, a black comedy, the most.
10. Erin was born in Kelowna, British Columbia, wasn't she?

9 Quotation Marks

1. Kathy Norris claims, "In spite of the cost of living, it's still popular."
2. One time the police stopped me for speeding, and they said, "Don't you know the speed limit is 55 miles per hour?" I said, "Yeah, I know, but I wasn't gonna' be out that long."
3. "It is not the strongest of the species that survive, nor the most intelligent," Charles Darwin said, "but the one most responsive to change."
4. Brian Kiley announced, "I went to a bookstore the other day. I asked the woman behind the counter where the self-help section was. She said, 'If I told you that, it would defeat the whole purpose.'"
5. "Last night," Ron Fairly stated during on-air coverage of a San Francisco Giants game, "I neglected to mention something that bears repeating."
6. "This taught me a lesson, but I'm not sure what it is," John McEnroe once stated after losing a championship game.
7. Albert Szent-Gyorgyi points out that discovery is nothing more than "an accident meeting a prepared mind."
8. "I merely took the energy it takes to pout," Duke Ellington said, "and wrote some blues."

9. "Proofreading is like scrimshaw," James J. Kilpatrick laments. "It is getting to be a lost art."
10. Peter de Vries loves being a writer, even though he "can't stand the paperwork."

18 Commas, Colons, and Semicolons (Answers may vary.)

1. Great assets are talent, intelligence, facility, and opportunity.
2. When your habits reflect your intentions, the world will see you as yourself.
3. Failure, like success, is the result of an attempt.
4. Don't regret your mistakes; instead, regret your missed opportunities to correct them.
5. Carl Jung said, "The meeting of two personalities is like the contact of two chemical substances: if there is any reaction, both are transformed."
6. Govern a family as you would fry small fish: gently.
7. A divorce is like an amputation: you survive, but there's less of you.
8. Writing is the only thing that when I do it, I don't feel I should be doing something else.
9. To be loved, be lovable.
10. I see but one rule: To be clear. If I am not clear, all my world crumbles to nothing.

24 Apostrophes

1. I'd like to know whose idea it was to change the rules, probably someone's brother-in-law.
2. Changing grammar rules sounds like something from the 1960s.
3. I'm surprised they didn't decide to do away with quotation marks while they were at it.
4. It's a good thing they haven't tried to legislate other grammar rules.
5. Apostrophes cause writers headaches! After a while, it looks like all the s's need one.
6. Jess's and Tom's essays show the boys' trouble with apostrophes may never end.
7. It's really not as difficult as it looks; with a few hours' practice, most people can understand the rules.
8. Just remember, look for missin' letters and words that show possession.
9. Jess and Tom's teacher has answered their apostrophe questions.
10. It's hotter now than it was in the early '50s.

33 Punctuation

1. Some of the smaller cities in Colorado—Colorado Springs, Pueblo, and Grand Junction—resent paying for roads in Denver when improvements are also needed in these smaller cities.

 ECS Learning Systems, Inc.

2. Consequently, rush hour traffic has grown into an unbearable snarl in Colorado Springs, according to regular commuters.
3. But maybe it's a blessing in disguise; better roads bring more people, and the smaller cities are already growing fast enough.
4. Even if the state has no money to expand the highway system, the forty-year-old road system in Colorado still needs an overhaul.
5. Potholes, narrow bridges, and too few lanes all create hazards for even wary travelers.
6. If drivers are lucky enough to avoid accidents, they still risk blowing tires and wrecking alignments on the hazard-packed highways.
7. The Colorado Highway Department claims that they have a greater disadvantage over most states: they have to build mountains roads.
8. Mountain highways can cost twenty-five times as much as building highways on the plains, which puts pressure on the ever-shrinking construction dollar.
9. Add this to the state's much admired determination to restore the surrounding land back to its original state, and it's no wonder the rest of the state feels cheated.
10. One legislator, who is not known as a defender of the environment, complained that "taking the land back to its original state is bad enough, but do we have to make it even better than it was? That's outrageously expensive!"

42   Capitalization and Punctuation

1. We sailed on the Sea of Cortéz over Christmas vacation last year.
2. Amy's dad bought a new car this summer, a Dodge minivan.
3. Jess is taking English, Spanish, Algebra 201, biology, and band.
4. The class wanted French fries at their Spanish fiesta.
5. The teacher said, "Please read *Tales From the Crypt* for Halloween."
6. The principal at Broadmoor Elementary has Swedish-design furniture.
7. The Catholic church just west of us is having a Good Friday service.
8. Jayne's stockbroker increased the value of her Gateway computer stock portfolio by 20% this year.
9. Eli put up a Christmas tree this year even though he's Jewish.
10. My uncle was elected to the Colorado Senate this year.

My hair began to turn gray the year my boys, Jess and Dusty, turned four and two. Jess took his job as older brother very seriously and constantly made helpful suggestions to Dusty, who, at half Jess' age, only had half of his life experience, wisdom, and common sense. Jess encouraged Dusty to swing from the living room curtains, scale the refrigerator by way of the microwave, and "chug" the tomato plants in the garden. The last item Jess announced as I was hosing down the kitchen after the boys had finished a spaghetti lunch: "Dusty and I chugged all the tomatoes for you, Mommy." I was quite pleased to discover that, already at four, Jess could conjugate the verb he had made up.

ECS Learning Systems, Inc.   The Grammar Notebook

When I asked him what "chugged" meant, I was less thrilled to discover that "chug" meant "yank out of the ground and throw in a pile." What was a mother to do?

My friends with little girls casually shared that their little girls still took morning naps. Their little girls loved to help fold laundry. Their little girls could sit quietly for hours with nothing more than a coloring book and a box of crayons—which of course were all still wrapped in their papers. Although my friends never said it, I suspected that they suspected my boys were victims of sloppy, free-for-all parenting. Who knows? They may have been right. During those years, it just didn't seem fair that my friends with girls had time to bake cookies and read magazines, while I stayed buried under a laundry mountain of lunch-stained T-shirts.

Somewhere about the time our children started school, though, the tables began to shift. Now my friends wailed, "My little girl comes home at least once a week in tears because this friend or that said she hates her. Last week she cried for an hour because she was teased for having a purple lunch box instead of a pink one. Girls can be so vicious!" Having once been a young girl myself, I would agree. Being the mother of two boys means I rarely, if ever, have to deal with tears and trauma. And I've certainly never had to comfort them over the color of a lunch box. I guess life has a way of evening things out. Thank goodness!

57   Commonly Confused Words

1. It's going to be too hot to be comfortable today.
2. There won't be any way to cool off except to go swimming.
3. A lot of the kids in the neighborhood have already decided to go to the pool.
4. They're planning a big party to celebrate the end of summer.
5. It's altogether possible that it will last past midnight.
6. Everyone is assigned a food to bring.
7. There could have been a problem with this.
8. But the mom who's in charge of the planning has done this a lot.
9. She's always thorough and really careful about who brings what.
10. It's certainly all right with everyone that she takes on the responsibility.